SportsZone Biographies

ALEX MORGAN

BY Luke Hanlon

SportsZone

An Imprint of Abdo Publishing
abdobooks.com

Published by Abdo Publishing, a division of ABDO, PO Box 398166, Minneapolis, Minnesota 55439. Copyright © 2024 by Abdo Consulting Group, Inc. International copyrights reserved in all countries. No part of this book may be reproduced in any form without written permission from the publisher. SportsZone™ is a trademark and logo of Abdo Publishing.

Printed in the United States of America, North Mankato, Minnesota.
052023
092023

Cover Photo: Colin E. Braley/AP Images
Interior Photos: Robert Cianflone/Getty Images Sport/Getty Images, 5; Catherine Ivill/ FIFA/Getty Images, 6; Paul Chinn/The San Francisco Chronicle/Hearst Newspapers/ Getty Images, 9; Santiago Llanquin/AP Images, 11; Roberto Candia/AP Images, 12; Mike Zarrilli/Getty Images Sport/Getty Images, 15; Friedemann Vogel/Getty Images Sport/ Getty Images, 16; Jonathan Hayward/The Canadian Press/AP Images, 19; David Klein/ SPORTIMAGE/Cal Sport Media/AP Images, 21; Dennis Grombkowski/Getty Images Sport/ Getty Images, 23; Christopher Lee/Getty Images Sport/Getty Images, 25; Quality Sport Images/Getty Images Sport/Getty Images, 26; Rich Graessle/Icon Sportswire/AP Images, 29

Editors: Steph Giedd and Charlie Beattie
Series Designer: Karli Kruse

LIBRARY OF CONGRESS CONTROL NUMBER: 2022949091

Publisher's Cataloging-in-Publication Data

Names: Hanlon, Luke, author.
Title: Alex Morgan / by Luke Hanlon
Description: Minneapolis, Minnesota: Abdo Publishing Company, 2024 | Series: SportsZone biographies | Includes online resources and index.
Identifiers: ISBN 9781098291662 (lib. bdg.) | ISBN 9781098278212 (ebook)
Subjects: LCSH: Morgan, Alex (Alexandra Patricia), 1989--Juvenile literature. | Soccer players--Biography--Juvenile literature. | Women soccer players--Biography--Juvenile literature. | Professional athletes--Biography--Juvenile literature.
Classification: DDC 796.092--dc23

TABLE OF CONTENTS

Chapter One

AMERICAN GIRL

Some people receive presents on their birthday. Alex Morgan gave one to her country. The star striker for the US Women's National Team (USWNT) was far from home on July 2, 2019. But there was nowhere she would have rather been on her 30th birthday.

The Women's World Cup is the pinnacle of women's soccer. The sport's greatest players come together every four years for the tournament that features the top national teams from around the globe. No country had won the Women's World Cup more than the United States. Morgan had been part of the USWNT's third championship team in 2015. Now she was ready to win another.

The United States had gotten off to a dominant start at the 2019 World Cup in France. The Americans had won their group, then defeated Spain and France in the knockout round. That set up a semifinal clash against England. It would

Alex Morgan celebrates after scoring a goal during the 2019 World Cup.

be the toughest test yet. England had won its last two games by 3–0 scores. But it hadn't played a team as strong as the USWNT.

The teams traded goals early. Just over 30 minutes had passed when US midfielder Lindsey Horan received a pass a few yards outside England's penalty area. She turned quickly to get a sight of England's goal. When Horan looked up, she saw Morgan with her hand in the air. Morgan made a run through the center of the English defense. Horan played a perfect cross to Morgan, who headed home the go-ahead goal.

Morgan ran with her hands in the air in celebration. Once she stopped running, she put her right hand to her mouth and mimed

Morgan's tea-sipping celebration against England was one of the most talked about moments of the 2019 World Cup.

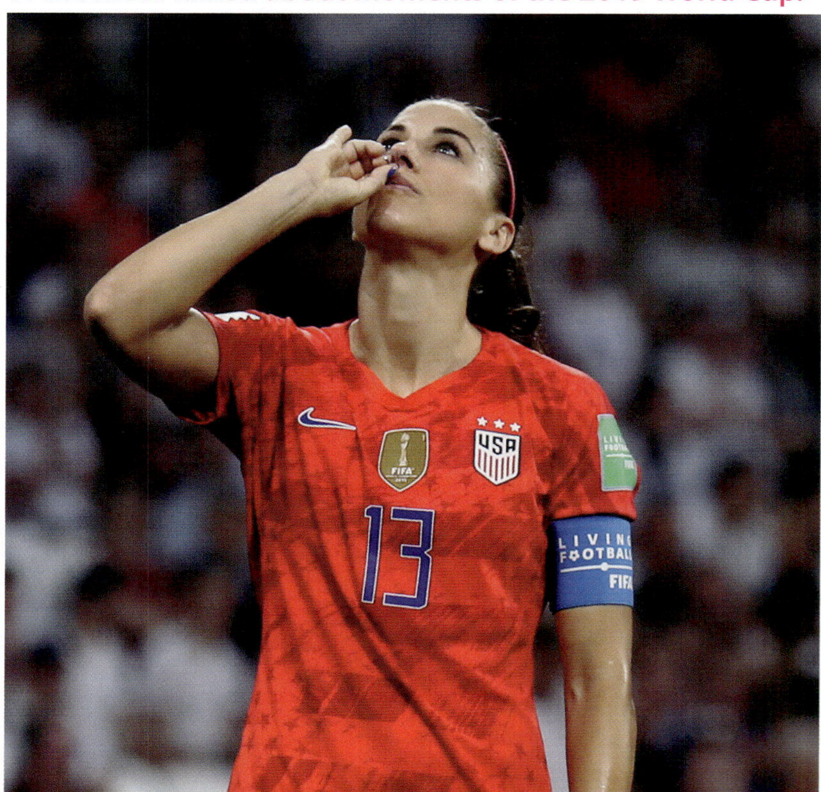

as if she was taking a sip of tea. The drink has been popular in England for hundreds of years. It's a staple of British culture. Many English fans and media members thought the celebration was disrespectful. Morgan said she performed that celebration because she "wanted to keep it interesting." Morgan also mentioned the celebration was a tribute to *Game of Thrones* star Sophie Turner. The actress often ends videos posted on her social media by saying "And that's the tea." The word *tea* in this case is slang for gossip or rumors.

Alex Morgan's goal against England was her sixth of the World Cup. Nobody scored more goals in the tournament. However, England's Ellen White and the USWNT's Megan Rapinoe each scored six goals as well.

No matter Morgan's intentions, that goal was enough for the Americans to win 2–1. Five days later, they defeated the Netherlands in the final. Morgan was a world champion once again.

CALIFORNIA KID

Morgan was born and raised in the suburbs of Los Angeles. She played several sports as a kid, including soccer. However, she didn't start playing competitive club soccer until she was 14. That put her behind other kids who had been playing on club teams for years.

But Morgan's natural ability quickly made her a star. Those skills carried over to Diamond Bar High School. There she was named an All-American.

Morgan stayed in her home state for college, heading north to the University of California, Berkeley. She excelled for the Golden Bears. Morgan led the team in goals all four years, and the team made the National Collegiate Athletic Association (NCAA) tournament each season she was there.

Morgan had her best season at California, Berkeley as a senior in 2010. She led the team with 14 goals despite appearing in only 12 matches. Morgan finished her college career with 45 goals, the third most in the school's history. She might have scored more and finished as UC Berkeley's all-time leading goal scorer, but she missed multiple games each season while playing for the youth and senior national teams. That international experience would soon pay off in a big way.

Morgan, *left*, protects the ball while playing for Cal–Berkeley against rival Stanford in 2008.

Chapter Two

ON THE WORLD STAGE

American soccer legends Mia Hamm, Joy Fawcett, and Julie Foudy all played their final game for the national team in 2004. The match was played in Carson, California. Alex Morgan attended the game as a fan, and she said that inspired her to pursue a soccer career.

Morgan's first international soccer experience came in the summer of 2008 while she was still in college. Though just 17 years old, she was called up to the US Under-20 (U-20) Women's National Team. Her first game came in the North American U-20 Women's Championship.

It didn't take long for Morgan to make an impact. The forward scored just minutes into her second game. The United States made the final of that tournament before losing to Canada. However, a bigger opportunity awaited Morgan and her American teammates later that year.

Morgan races after the ball against a North Korean defender during the U-20 World Cup Final in 2008.

Morgan, *right*, kisses the U-20 World Cup trophy as US coach Tony DiCicco celebrates.

The U-20 Women's World Cup was held that November in Chile. Morgan scored the first goal of the tournament for the United States on the way to beating France 3–0. She followed that with a two-goal performance against Argentina in another 3–0 win. But Morgan saved her best for the biggest stage.

The Americans faced North Korea in the final. With the US team already up 1–0, Morgan added to the lead in the 42nd minute. She received the ball with her back turned to the goal.

Once she turned, she beat two defenders before cutting to her
left, into the middle of the field. Another defender was about
to cut Morgan off, but she ripped a shot from just outside the
penalty area while falling over. Despite being off-balance,
Morgan managed to place her shot perfectly into the top corner.
The laser-like shot was voted the goal of the tournament. More
importantly, it helped secure a 2–1 win and a U-20 World Cup title
for the United States.

SUPER SUB

In March 2010, before Morgan's
senior season at UC Berkeley,
she earned her first call-up to
the USWNT. That November, the
team still had to beat Italy in a
two-legged playoff to qualify
for the 2011 World Cup. The first
game was in Italy, and Morgan
was subbed into the game in the
86th minute. She was only on
the field for about eight minutes, but she made a huge impact. In
the fourth minute of stoppage time, one of Morgan's teammate's
flicked a header behind the Italian defenders and into the penalty
area. Morgan sprinted after it, then composed herself while two
defenders closed in. Her shot into the far corner gave the United

States an important 1–0 victory. The Americans went on to win the second game as well, clinching their spot. Before the World Cup that summer, Morgan started playing professionally. The Western New York Flash took Morgan with the first overall pick in the 2011 Women's Professional Soccer (WPS) Draft. Morgan went on to score four goals in 14 matches with the Flash. Once again, her national team commitments cost her a few games. This time she was headed to the World Cup in Germany.

At 21 years old, Morgan was the youngest player on the US roster. Because she was among so many greats, such as Abby Wambach, Morgan was a bench player throughout the tournament. But she was eventually able to make her mark. The Americans dramatically beat Brazil in a shootout in the quarterfinals. That set up a semifinal matchup with France, and Morgan was subbed into the game in the 55th minute. She scored her first World Cup goal 26 minutes later to help the United States win 3–1.

As in the U-20 World Cup final in 2008, Morgan was at her best again in the biggest game. She came off the bench at the

Morgan poses with fans after a game while playing for the Western New York Flash in 2011.

start of the second half against Japan. In the 69th minute, Megan Rapinoe sent a long ball forward from deep within the United States' half. Morgan shrugged off a Japanese defender as she ran onto the ball. Upon entering the penalty area, she then hammered home a left-foot shot to put the Americans up 1–0.

Morgan, *left*, and teammate Abby Wambach celebrate Morgan's goal against Japan in the 2011 World Cup Final.

The lead didn't last, however. After Japan tied the game and sent it to extra time, Morgan stepped up again. She picked up a loose ball in the left corner, then delivered a cross to the front of the goal. Wambach was waiting for it, and she headed it home.

The game still wasn't over, though. Japan fought back to tie the game and eventually won in a shootout. Despite the loss, Morgan proved she belonged on the field with the greatest players in the world. The following January, she finished eighth in the voting for the 2011 FIFA World Player of the Year.

Morgan authored a four-book series titled *The Kicks* in 2013. The series featured four young girls learning about friendship and leadership through soccer. The series was developed into a streaming series on Amazon Prime Video in 2015. The 12th book in the series came out in 2021.

Chapter Three

GOLDEN GOAL

Alex Morgan and the USWNT didn't have to wait four years to avenge their heartbreaking loss to Japan. The sport's other biggest tournament, the Olympic Games, was set for the next year in London, England. The United States had dominated the competition since Women's soccer was added to the Games in 1996, winning three of four gold medals.

Morgan tallied two goals in the first match against France. She then picked up an assist in each of the team's next three games. The USWNT won all four games, which set up a semifinal matchup against North American rival Canada. Christine Sinclair, a teammate of Morgan's on the Western New York Flash, was Canada's star. The striker scored a hat trick. But each time she scored, the United States answered with a goal of its own. That sent the game to extra time. After 120 minutes, the game was still tied 3–3. The match looked as if it were heading to a penalty shootout.

Morgan celebrates her goal in a 2012 Olympic qualifying match against Canada with teammates Megan Rapinoe, *left*, and Lori Lindsey.

However, US midfielder Heather O'Reilly delivered a cross from outside the right side of the penalty box. Morgan was ready and jumped over a Canadian defender to get to the ball first. Her header went over the goalkeeper's outstretched hand and into the back of the net with just seconds left to play. Teammates mobbed Morgan in celebration, knowing her goal was enough to send them to the gold-medal match.

The Americans faced Japan with a chance to avenge their loss in the World Cup final the year prior. Morgan helped the Americans get off to a fast start, as she assisted Carli Lloyd's opening goal in the eighth minute. Lloyd added another goal in the second half, which proved to be enough. The United States won 2–1, and Morgan won her first major championship with the senior national team.

NEW BEGINNINGS

Despite playing alongside legends such as Lloyd, Megan Rapinoe, and Abby Wambach, Morgan was the USWNT's most prolific player in 2012. She led the team in both goals and assists that year. Morgan also became the first American player to have more than 20 goals and 20 assists in a single year since Mia Hamm in 1998.

Morgan provided an assist for one of the United States' two goals in its gold-medal match win against Japan at the 2012 Summer Olympics in London.

Morgan's club career took a step forward in 2013. Women's Professional Soccer had folded after the 2011 season. The National Women's Soccer League (NWSL) began playing in 2013. That year, Morgan once again joined forces with Sinclair, as the two forwards played for the Portland Thorns. The duo tied for the team lead in goals, scoring eight apiece. Morgan assisted a Sinclair goal in the league final against their former team, the Flash, helping the Thorns win the inaugural NWSL championship.

At the age of 23, Morgan had won a U-20 World Cup, an Olympic gold medal, and a league title in two different leagues. The one trophy missing from her collection was a World Cup at the senior level. But when she suffered a knee injury while playing for the Thorns in April 2015, it looked as if Morgan might miss that summer's World Cup.

However, Morgan recovered in time to make the USWNT roster. She made her first start of the tournament in a 1–0 win over Nigeria, which sent the United States to the knockout rounds. She scored her only goal of the tournament in the next game, a 2–0 win over Colombia.

Even though she was still recovering from the injury, Morgan started all four knockout-round games. That included the final against Japan. This final was far less dramatic than the first meeting in 2011. The United States won 5–2 to secure its first world title in 16 years. And Morgan got her hands on the trophy for the first time.

Morgan, *top*, celebrates with the USWNT after winning the 2015 World Cup Final over Japan.

Chapter Four

WINNING WAYS

Alex Morgan continued playing in the NWSL after the 2015 World Cup. But she decided to switch things up at the beginning of 2017, signing with powerhouse Olympique Lyonnais in Lyon, France. Morgan's stint with the club was short, as she appeared in 15 matches over a six-month span. However, she still achieved quite a bit during that time.

Morgan scored 12 goals in those 15 matches. And she helped the club win the top French league title, the French League Cup, and the Union of European Women's Champions League. The tournament pits the best club teams from different European countries against each other. It was another impressive addition to Morgan's trophy case.

After her time playing for Lyon, Morgan returned to France when the country hosted the 2019 World Cup. The United States was the team to beat after winning in 2015.

Morgan played in only 15 matches for Olympique Lyonnais in 2017, but she helped the club win a Champions League title.

Morgan and the Americans were ready for the pressure that comes with being defending champions.

The USWNT opened against Thailand. Morgan scored the opening goal in the 12th minute. She then assisted on the second US goal. Then, in the second half, she really went off. Morgan added four goals and two assists in the final 45 minutes. She ended the game with five goals and three assists, and the United States won 13–0. That was the largest margin of victory in the history of

Morgan poses with her collection of trophies after the United States defeated the Netherlands in the 2019 World Cup Final.

either the men's or women's World Cup. The USWNT's remaining games in the tournament were much closer. But the Americans won every game they played on their way to back-to-back world titles.

FIGHTING FOR EQUALITY

The 2019 team was again honored with a parade through New York City. Parades are meant for partying and celebrating a team's success. The parade in 2019 was about more than that, however. Fans throughout the day chanted, "Equal pay!" Signs were posted on building windows saying the same thing. That was because players on the USWNT were paid $90,000 for making the World Cup. Players on the men's national team were paid $550,000 for the same feat.

Pay gaps between men and women are common in soccer. Morgan and other USWNT teammates tried to change that for American soccer in 2019. Members of the women's team filed a lawsuit claiming they were unfairly paid less than the men. The suit started a long legal battle. Finally, in 2022, the

United States Soccer Federation settled with the USWNT for a total of $24 million. The agreement also ensured that the men's and women's teams would be paid equally for all future competitions.

HOME SWEET HOME

Morgan's club career saw her play in Rochester, New York, Portland, Orlando, and multiple European clubs. Before the 2022 NWSL season, Morgan moved back to California and signed with the San Diego Wave, a new team that season. The move worked out well for Morgan, as she scored a league-high 15 goals in 17 regular-season games, earning her the NWSL Golden Boot award for the 2022 season. And in the playoffs, Morgan scored a key extra-time goal to help the Wave win in the quarterfinals.

Morgan did all that while suffering from a recurring knee injury that kept her out of USWNT action. Of course, it wasn't the first time she had dealt with adversity in her long and stellar career. And every time, Morgan seemed to bounce back better than ever. Her fans hoped she could do it again.

Morgan gave birth to her daughter Charlie in May 2020. Becoming a mother kept Morgan off the field for 15 months. Her first game back was in November 2020 while playing the 2020–21 season for the English club Tottenham Hotspur.

Morgan led the San Diego Wave to the NWSL semifinals in 2022.

GLOSSARY

assist
A pass that leads directly to
a goal.

cross
A pass delivered from the side
of the field toward the middle.

draft
A system that allows teams to
acquire new players coming
into a league.

extra time
Two 15-minute periods added
to a game if the score is tied at
the end of regulation.

hat trick
Three or more goals by the
same player in one game.

knockout
A kind of competition in which
one loss eliminates a team.

lawsuit
A claim in a court of law.

shootout
A series of penalty kicks held
after extra time to decide who
wins a tie game.

striker
A player whose primary
responsibility is to create
scoring chances and
score goals.

BOOKS

Flynn, Brendan. *Girls' Soccer*. Minneapolis, MN: Abdo Publishing, 2022.

Hewson, Anthony K. *GOATs of Soccer*. Minneapolis, MN: Abdo Publishing, 2022.

Marthaler, Jon. *Ultimate Soccer Road Trip*. Minneapolis, MN: Abdo Publishing, 2019.

ONLINE RESOURCES

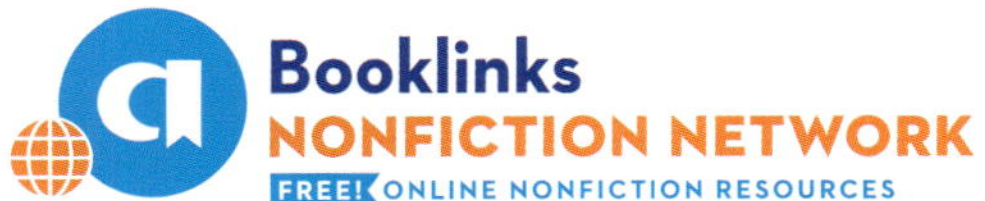

To learn more about Alex Morgan, please visit **abdobooklinks.com** or scan this QR code. These links are routinely monitored and updated to provide the most current information available.

ABOUT THE AUTHOR

Luke Hanlon is a sportswriter and editor based in Minneapolis.